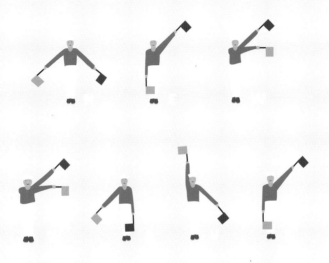

NEW WAVE FACTS ABOUT FLAGS

**black dog
publishing**

london uk

CONTENTS

70 PROTEST FLAGS

84 FLAG ETIQUETTE

94 FLAGS AT SEA

108 SPORTS FLAGS

116 POPULAR CULTURE

128 SOVEREIGN FLAGS

138 FLAG TERMS

THE HISTORY OF THE FLAG

FOR YOU ARE THE MAKERS OF THE FLAG AND IT IS WELL THAT YOU GLORY IN THE MAKING.

Franklin Knight Lane

The evolution of the flag can be traced alongside the history of mankind, as it developed from a symbol of hierarchy to one of recognition and collective identity. Humans have for centuries rallied around flags and their diverse symbolism and this trait is sure to exist into the future as flags and the meanings associated with them continue to diversify.

The earliest known usage of proto-flags can be dated back to prehistoric times, where mankind developed as communal groups,

Eagles have been popular vexillogical symbols for centuries.

hunting and living in tribes. As natural leaders emerged from these groups, ways in which to identify these individuals developed–often by ceremonial dress and the carrying of spears decorated with emblems. This proto-flag is known as a vexilloid, and its symbolism can be seen in ancient examples of Aztec vexilloids.

As time passed on, ancient civilisations across the world began to develop the use of the flag. Ancient Egyptian vexilloids show provinces of a pre-dynastic

Ancient vexilloids representing the provinces of pre-dynastic Egypt.

Examples of classic ancient Chinese banners.

The Romans copied the use of bearing vexilloids from the Persians, who carried a large standard with a fringed square cloth hanging from a crossbar, fastened beneath the spear top of their lance. The famous Eagle emblem borne by the Romans was also appropriated from the Persians. Later, the *draco* (dragon flag) became popular in Rome; this features a hollow bronze dragons' head with a serpent-like windsock attached. In the sixth century the *draco* was adopted by Saxon conquerors and used by Anglo-Saxon and Norman armies until the twelfth century.

Egypt, and many examples of early Egyptian proto-flags show emblems of their gods. The first banners began to emerge when silk was invented in ancient China. These banners were easier to carry than prehistoric or Egyptian vexilloids and could be seen from a much greater distance. The Chinese were the first to use fabric in their flags, which they attached sideways to staffs, much like the majority of common flags today. Initially, these Chinese flags were mostly banner-like in shape, but they later developed into squares or triangles, often with flammules (flame shaped edges). From China, this practice spread to Mongolia, India, Persia, and then to Europe through the Roman Empire.

The oldest visual references to flags come from frescoes found in the Roman city of Paestum, where images of Samnite soldiers depict them carrying flags.

From the late eighth century, the Vikings became the first Europeans to consistently use flags at sea. Viking flags were triangular and rounded at the edge. The Vikings had many different flags, but the most important was probably the raven flag, which appeared on many Viking coins from the beginning of the tenth century. The Bayeux tapestry depicts a flag similar to the raven flag being carried by a soldier behind William the Conqueror.

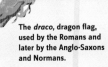

The *draco*, dragon flag, used by the Romans and later by the Anglo-Saxons and Normans.

7

Most of the banners depicted in the tapestry bear a cross, a symbol of the military and seamen in pre-heraldic times.

Banners emblazoned with a cross were also widely used in The First Crusade, 1096-1099. The invention of the helmet to cover and protect the faces of warriors meant that the use of flags for identification became far more important, so that by the twelfth century vexilloids changed from purely ceremonial or military symbols to tools to indicate rulers, domains and nationality.

The Cross banner, a popular flag used during the First Crusade.

Representaion of the Raven flag used by the Vikings.

The Second Crusade, 1147-1149, saw the widespread adoption of the basic rules of heraldry, and knights returning from the Crusades took these customs back to their home countries. Popular heraldic imagery included crosses, lions, eagles, griffins, horses, *fleur-de-lis*, roses and various weapons. Heraldry helped to distinguish flags depicting hierarchy, as well as leading to a rapid growth in personal flags attaining to individual identity.

With the Mongol conquest of China in 1279 the design of flags in that part of the world changed. Mongol flags were typically triangular, with flammules, and in the instance of the flag of Genghis Khan, flames were added to the trident and horses' tails were attached to the base.

In Europe, the display of heraldic banners was important in the battlefield, but also in the jousting tournaments which became hugely popular between the thirteenth and sixteenth centuries. These tournaments gave knights from all over Europe the opportunity to display, through their individual coats of arms, their skill in handling horses and weapons.

The general use of armourial banners began to fade during the sixteenth century. Flags displayed at sea during this time generally consisted of a single coloured flag field bearing a symbol of arms.

The first national flags on land began to emerge in the late eighteenth century, as did yachting club flags. One of the first national flags was the Dutch revolutionary *Prinsenvlag*, composed of single horizontal stripes rather than heraldic devices–flags created after other revolutions in America and France followed a similar design. The most popular symbol of early national flags was a five-pointed star, which was a symbol of liberty and independence.

Between the nineteenth and twentieth centuries, the use of flags became more widespread throughout society. Flags could represent government agencies, provinces, rankings in the armed forces, schools, organisations or guerrilla movements. Modern sovereign flags reflect the many political changes of the nineteenth and twentieth centuries, where revolutions replaced monarchist rule and national flag design was used to reflect the political and ideological messages of countries. Sovereign flags have thus become massively important for a sense of national identity, or indeed symbolic of a lack of this.

The Dutch revolutionary *Prinsenvlag*, one of the first national flags.

Flags can symbolise loyalty, ideology, anarchy, geography, pride, liberty, power, anger, personality and history. So much can be said and understood through the design of a flag, and indeed by the bearing, following or rejection of it. Flags have such a great prominence in contemporary society that in many ways they have become the defining symbol of identity; what each flag represents, though, is inevitably subjective. Flags will, however, continue to represent the aspirations and beliefs of humankind for centuries to come, as they have done throughout the course of history.

FLAG CHARGES

A charge is any object, figure or symbol appearing on a flag, with most contemporary sovereign flags displaying them. The most popular charges are based on a simple division of straight lines within a flag's field, the most common being cantons, stars, bends, crosses, triangles and piles.

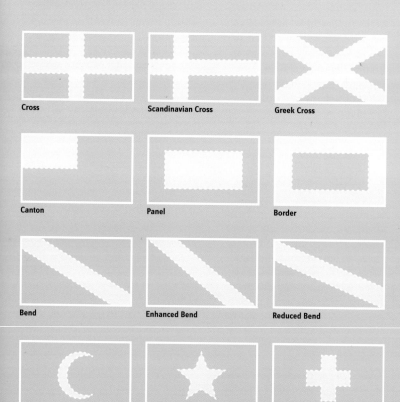

Cross

Scandinavian Cross

Greek Cross

Canton

Panel

Border

Bend

Enhanced Bend

Reduced Bend

Crecent

Star

Saltire

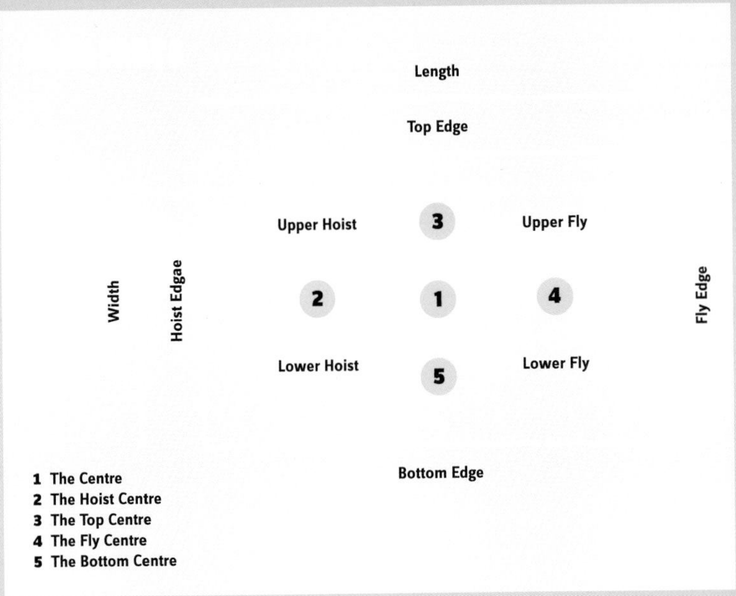

Length

Top Edge

Upper Hoist **3** Upper Fly

Width Hoist Edgae **2** **1** **4** Fly Edge

Lower Hoist **5** Lower Fly

Bottom Edge

1 The Centre
2 The Hoist Centre
3 The Top Centre
4 The Fly Centre
5 The Bottom Centre

Triangle

Pile

Trapezium

Upright Triangle

Inverted Pile

Upright Pile

Upright Chevron

Chevron

Lozenge

FLAG DIVISIONS

Flags can be proportionally divided into various sections, which inform typical structures of flag design. Divisions in the field of a flag can be horizontal or vertical–known as stripes; ordiagonal–known as bends. If these intersections are of equal size then only the number of them is necessary in a flags description. If they are unequal, then the proportionate width of each section must be quoted to indicate the design.

Horizontally

Vertically

Quarterly

Horizontally Twice

Vertically Twice

Checky

Diagonally

Diagonally to Left

Per Saltire

Diagonally Twice

Diagonally Twice to Left

Gyronny

FLAG RATIOS

Different countries use different measures of width (upper to lower edge) and length (pole end to fly end) for their flags. The ratio 13:15 is used in the Belgian flag; 28:37 is used in Denmark; the US typically uses 2:3 or 3:5 ratios; and the UK and historic Soviet flags use a ratio of 1:2.

FLAG SHAPES

Flags are typically recognised as being rectangular in shape, and though this is true of most modern flags, triangular shapes and flammules are still used in some instances, as are longer banner shapes. Historically, flags were less rigidly proportioned and would often have streamers, curved edges or cut out sections. This reflects the changing usage of flags, as in centuries past they were used as totems of war and conquest, whilst today they are typically symbols of identity.

HISTORICAL

Gonfanon

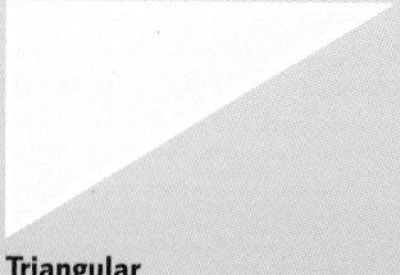

Triangular

Schwenkel

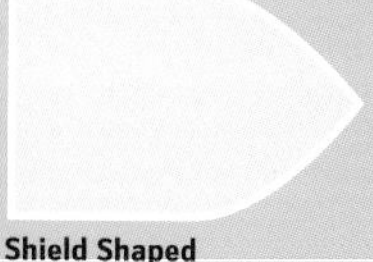

Shield Shaped

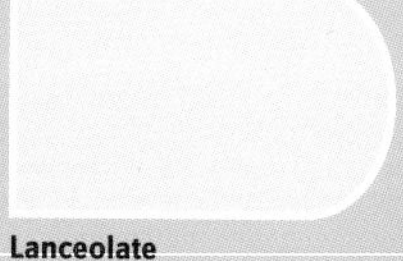

Lanceolate

Descate

Double-tailed Descate

Windsock

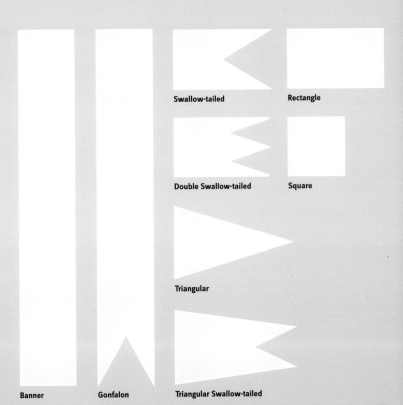

Swallow-tailed

Rectangle

Double Swallow-tailed

Square

Triangular

Banner

Gonfalon

Triangular Swallow-tailed

HOISTS

The term "hoist" refers to the way in which a flag is attached to a flagpole or flagstaff and raised. A hoist is the section of the flag nearest the pole. When hoisting a flag, the halyard–or rope–is typically woven into the heading and grommets through the toggle at the top and the becket at the bottom. There are many other ways of hoisting flags, as detailed below.

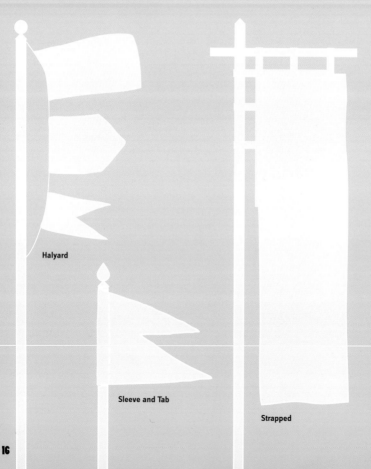

Halyard

Sleeve and Tab

Strapped

Frame Attachment

Halyard
and Bar

Ring Frame

Western European
and Latin American
Halyard

COLOURS

RED

RED OFTEN REPRESENTS COURAGE AND REVOLUTION, AS IT DID ON THE FLAG OF THE SOVIET UNION...

USSR

AS WELL AS HARDINESS AND VALOUR AS IT DOES ON THE FLAG OF THE USA.

USA

BLUE

BLUE CAN REPRESENT WATER, OCEANS AND WATERWAYS AS IT DOES IN THE FLAGS OF SOMALIA AND ISRAEL...

Israel

AS WELL AS FREEDOM AND LIBERTY AS IT DOES ON THE FRENCH FLAG.

Somalia

France

YELLOW

YELLOW OFTEN REPRESENTS THE SUN, WEALTH AND PROSPERITY AS EXEMPLIFIED IN THE FLAG OF COLOMBIA AND IN PAN-AFRICAN FLAGS SUCH AS THAT OF MALI.

Mali

Colombia

GREEN

GREEN CAN SYMBOLISE THE EARTH AND AGRICULTURE, SUCH AS ON THE JAMAICAN FLAG, AND THE MUSLIM FAITH AS FOUND ON THE FLAG OF PAKISTAN.

Jamaica

Pakistan

WHITE

WHITE EVOKES THE WINTER SNOWS IN THE FINNISH FLAG, WHILE IN SINGAPORE WHITE REPRESENTS EVERLASTING PURITY.

Finland

Singapore

ORANGE

ORANGE IN THE INDIAN FLAG REPRESENTS HINDUISM, WHILE IN ARMENIA IT SYMBOLISES CROPS AND A GOOD HARVEST.

India

Armenia

THE STORY OF THE AUSTRIAN AND GERMAN COLOURS

Legend says the red, white, red flag of modern Austria was born of the Crusades and the experiences of Duke Leopold V. After fighting in a particularly brutal battle, the Duke's white battle dress was covered in the blood of his enemies. However, when he removed his belt after the battle, the area underneath was completely untouched, resulting in a pattern of two bands of blood separated by clean white cloth. The Duke was so struck by the image that he adopted it as his banner and it has remained as the national flag of Austria ever since.

The colours of the German flag originated in the 'Freedom Wars' against Napoleon in 1813. These colours were worn by the Lützow Free Corps whose uniforms were black with red facings and gold buttons. The colour choice for the uniform was a pragmatic one; many of the soldiers were required to supply their own uniforms and it was easiest for them to dye clothes black. The colours of the uniform reflect the sentiment of the 'Freedom Wars': "Out of the blackness (black) of servitude through bloody (red) battles to the golden (gold) light of freedom."

THE STORY OF THE IRISH COLOURS

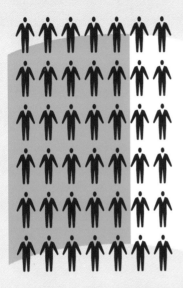

It is said that this tricolore first appeared in 1848 as a gift to Thomas Francis Meagher from sympathisers to the Irish cause, although it only made its appearance in the public arena in 1916 during the Irish rebellion against British rule that became known as the Easter Rising. Green represents the Catholic majority, orange the Protestant minority who sided with William of Orange, and white symbolises the union and peace between the two faiths. Green has a long-standing association with Ireland, particularly as it stands for its older majority Gaelic tradition.

NATIONAL FLAG STORIES
INDIA

The history of the Indian flag is largely derived from the country's former status as a British colony, its fight for independence and its position today as the most populated democracy in the world.

Before the British established the Indian Empire, there existed the Mughal Empire, which governed the majority of what is now the Indian subcontinent between around 1526 and 1858. The most widely used flag of the Moghal Empire was the Alam, which was allegedly the flag of the warrior Hussain.

When the British first established the British Raj in 1858–taking control of what is now modern-day India, Pakistan, Bangladesh and Burma–the Union Jack was adopted as the official state flag. From 1880, another semi-official land flag was also used at and by various events and associations. This second flag featured the Union Jack against a red ensign with the Order of the Star of India–an order of chivalry founded by Queen Victoria–in the fly.

The flag of Calcutta was one of the first unofficial flags of India that was created in direct response to a desire for independence from the British. A vertical tricolore, the flag design shows eight half-open lotus flowers along the orange strip, which together represent the eight provinces of India.

Top to bottom
The Alam, a flag of the Mughal Empire from 1526-1857.
The semi-official flag of British India from 1880-1947.
An early Indian nationalistic flag known as the flag of Calcutta, 1906.

27

The inscription quotes the poem "Vande Mataram", meaning, "I bow to thee, Mother", taken from a hymn to the goddess Durga, popularly seen as the national personification of India.

A decade later, the Indian Independence Movement was gaining momentum. The Home Rule League was established in 1916 as a national organisation aiming to lead the fight for self-government within the British-ruled Indian Empire. The flag features a Union Jack as the league wanted to establish a Dominion status, like other countries that were in the British Empire such as Australia. The seven white stars depict the Saptarishi constellation which is sacred to Hindus.

In 1921, Mohandas Karamchand Gandhi developed a flag that was intended to function as a national flag for independent India. The flag featured the symbol of the *charkha* (spinning wheel) which represented the Indian people's hope for self sufficiency. The colours depicted the main religious groups of India: Hinduism in red; Islam in green; and white to represent the other religious groups that comprised the nation. A development of Gandhi's flag, the Swaraj, was officially adopted by the Indian National Congress in 1931.

Top and bottom
Indian flag used by the All India Home Rule movement in 1917.
Flag designed by Ghandi in 1921.

The current Indian national flag is still very similar to the Swaraj flag and has been the official state flag since India first won its independence in 1947. The three colours of the tricolore stand for different traits important to the nation: orange for Hinduism, courage and sacrifice; white for the hope of peace; and green for chivalry, faith and Islam. The *chakra* represents the inevitability of existence; it is blue on the flag to depict the ocean and the sky, and the 24 spokes of the wheel represent the 24 hours of the day.

Top and bottom
The Ashoka Chakra, "the wheel of Righteousness", still used in the Indian national flag today.
The Swaraj flag, adopted by the Indian National Congress in 1931.

NATIONAL FLAG STORIES
CHINA

Dragons have been an important symbol in China for centuries and are believed to be bringers of good luck. The dragon was a symbol of the Emperor of the Zhou Dynasty, 1046 AD-256 BC, and was used in the latter part of the nineteenth century as the symbol of the Qing Dynasty–the last dynasty of Imperial China, 1644-1912. Although dragons are no longer represented in the flags of the People's Republic of China (PRC) they still hold strong cultural meanings, both in China and internationally as symbols of the nation.

The Republic of China (ROC) formed in 1912–following the fall of the Qing Dynasty and marking the end of 2,000 years of Imperial China–with a new flag representing the Republic's major principle of five races under one nation. The flag featured five multi-coloured stripes, each representing the five races of China: The Han (red); the Manchus (yellow); the Mongols (blue); the Muslims or "Hui" (white); and the Tibetans (black). Yuan Shikai–the first president of the ROC–placed the red Han symbol as a dominant saltire and then cross in the flag. Shikai's 'Empire' was however quickly dissolved as provinces across China rebelled against his rule.

The eventual reformation of the ROC in 1928 was marked with a new flag depicting a blue sky, white sun and red earth.

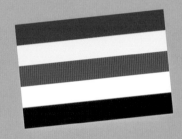

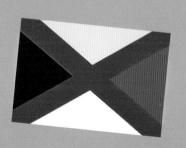

Top to bottom
Qing Dynasty flag in place from 1890-1912.
National Flag of the Republic of China 1912-1928.
Flag of Yuan Shikai's Empire of China, 1916.

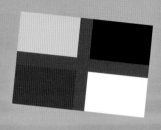

This flag is still used to represent nations in the ROC, such as Taiwan. The 12 rays of the sun represent the 12 hours of the clock, against which all progress is measured.

The flag of the ROC was also the party flag of the Kuomintang, the Chinese Nationalist Party that was in power from 1928-1949. With the rise to power of the Chinese Communist Party, and the establishment of the People's Republic of China (PRC), a new flag was again introduced. A newspaper competition invited people to design the flag for the PRC, which had to draw inspiration from Chinese geography, nationality, history, culture and communist ideals. Rectangular in shape, the flag was to measure a length-breadth ratio of 3:2 and had to be mainly bright red in colour. Around 3,000 designs for the flag were received. Mao Zedong and other party members initially preferred the 'Yellow River' flag, which featured a party star in the canton, with a golden strip across the flag representing the Yellow River, "the cradle of Chinese civilisation". It was ultimately decided, however, that the golden strip could also be seen as representing a division in the revolution and nation and Zeng Liansong's design was chosen instead as the new national flag of the PRC.

Top and bottom
Flag of Yuan Shikai's Empire of China, 1916.
Flag of the Republic of China
from 1928-1949.

Liansong's flag initially had a hammer and sickle in the canton, surrounded by four stars, but as this was seen as being too similar to the flag of the USSR it was replaced with a large five-pointed star. This represents communism and the party. The four stars surrounding this are symbolic of the four classes of the Chinese people as identified by Mao Zedong: workers, peasants, petty bourgeoisie and patriotic capitalists. The design has been maintained in the national flag of the PRC throughout its existence.

Top and bottom
Proposed design for the flag of The People's Republic of China, also known as the 'Yellow River' flag.
Zeng Liansong's original design for the flag of The People's Republic of China.

NATIONAL FLAG STORIES
IRAQ

The first Iraqi flag was inspired by the Arab Revolt, with the black, white, red and green colours that were used representing the Hashemite leaders of the Revolt and the two seven pointed white stars representing the Arabs and the Kurds. The flag was implemented in 1921 with the appointment of the first monarch of the Kingdom of Iraq and lasted until the 1958 Abdul Karim Qassim Revolution that removed the King from power.

A short-lived flag of the Arab Federation was adopted in 1958, representing a confederation of the kingdoms of Iraq and Jordan, although it did not even last the year as the flag was discarded when Iraq became a republic at the end of 1958. From here, a new flag was adopted–black and green for pan-Arabism with a yellow sun to represent the Kurdish minority of the country and a red star of Ishtar to represent the Assyrian minority. This flag is still flown today in certain parts of Kurdish Iraq.

When the Qassim government was overthrown in 1963, another new flag was introduced, this time including three green stars for the three tenets of the Ba'ath party motto "Wahda, Hurrigeh, Ishtirahiyah" or "Unity, Freedom, Socialism" and the red, white and black tricolore still featured in the design of the flag today.

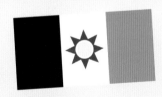

Top to bottom
First Iraqi flag, introduced in 1921.
The flag of the Arab Federation, adopted in 1958 for a short time.
The first flag of the Iraqi Republic, 1958-1963.

This flag was altered when Saddam Hussein came into power in 1991, when the *Takbir* ("Allaahu Akbar", or "God is Great") was added to the middle strip of the tricolore. The text of the Takbir was printed in the style of Hussein's own handwriting.

During the US-led invasion of Iraq, after the Americans 'took' Baghdad, soldiers famously covered the face of a statue of Hussein with an American flag. This was swiftly removed due to the controversy related to the symbolism it evoked and an old Iraqi flag was placed over the head in its place. An American military tank then tore down the statue and Iraqi citizens celebrating in the street hacked off the statue's head. The event, covered heavily in the media, convinced many dubious Westerners that Iraqi citizens wanted the American and Allied forces there and were grateful for the 'intervention'. However, reports have since claimed that the event was orchestrated by US intelligence in order to justify the invasion of Iraq, that crowd scenes were doctored to create a greater sense of support and that the flag itself, which would have been very hard to obtain at the time, was actually a plant.

Top and bottom
The flag representing the Ba'ath party motto, 1963-1991.
The flag bearing the Takbir in Saddam Hussein's handwriting, 1991-2004.

After the removal of Hussein and the appointment of the Iraqi Governing Council in 2004, it was announced that a new flag had been chosen from a competition. This design was greeted with controversy, as it moved away from the pan-Arab colours and the Muslim crescent was made light blue rather than traditional green or red. The flag was burned by protestors and the blue crescent flag was eventually abandoned due to the widespread negative response.

Currently, the official flag of Iraq is still in debate. Since 2008, the flag used has been the red, white and black tricolore with the Takbir, now written in traditional Kufic script. However, this is only intended to be an interim measure until a new official flag design is decided upon.

Top and bottom
The proposed blue crescent flag, 2004.
The current Iraqi flag, 2008-present, is only intended to be an interim measure until a permanant design is agreed upon.

NATIONAL FLAG STORIES
JAPAN

The sun disc Hinoramu flag–or *Nisshōki* (sun mark)–has been synonymous with Japan since 1870, though it was not officially adopted as the national flag until 1999. No previous legislation in Japan had specified a singular national flag, though the Hinomaru was widely regarded as Japan's sovereign symbol, both at home and abroad. The only alteration made to the flag in 1999 was a miniscule shift of the disc towards the hoist.

The symbolism of the sun disk has been integral throughout Japanese history; a Hinomaru was allegedly the symbol of Emperor Mommu, the 42nd Emperor of Japan. The oldest surviving flag–held in the Umpo-ji temple in Yamanashi– has been dated as pre-sixteenth century, though historical hearsay indicates that the flag could have been handed down through the dynasties from as far back as the eleventh century. Other Japanese myths propose that the Hinomaru symbolism originates from a thirteenth century story involving a Buddhist priest, who offered a sun disk flag to the Emperor in honour of his ancestor Amaterasu, the goddess of the sun in the Shinto faith.

Top to bottom
Flag of the Ryūkyū Kingdom, 1869–1875.
Flag of the Japanese Okinawa Prefecture.
Flag of the Japanese Kagoshima Prefecture.

The years of the Meji Restoration–which saw the reclamation of the Japanese empire–witnessed the popularisation of the now iconic sun disk Hinomaru flag and the Rising Sun flag of the Imperial Japanese Navy. The Japanese invaded the previously independent Ryūkyū Kingdom, which encompassed the modern day Okinawa Prefecture and the Kagoshima Prefecture–these areas remain a part of Japan today.

Other flags representing Japan were designed with similar aesthetics in mind to help enforce the sense of a unified Japanese Empire; the Standard of the Japanese Emperor is a classic example of this, featuring a similarly centred disk in gold against red and decorated with chrysanthemums–the public symbol of the Japanese Emperor since the twelfth century.

Propaganda posters, textbooks, and films depicted the flag as a source of pride to enforce a sense of national identity and patriotism in citizens of the empire. It was decreed that the flag must be flown in Japanese homes during national holidays, celebrations and other occasions as stipulated by the government.

Top and bottom
Standard of the Japanese
Emperor, 1869–present.
Flag of the Japanese
Hiroshima Prefecture.

Today, the flag is viewed as a powerful and enduring symbol of Japan, with many believing that nothing else could represent the nation as effectively. To others, it is an overly nationalistic and outdated denotation of the country, still contentious in certain areas and especially in Hiroshima due to its associations with the Second World War and the resulting US military presence in Japan. During the occupation of Japan–led by the US, with inclusions from Australia, India and New Zealand–the allied flag of Japan replaced the civil and naval ensign between 1945 and 1952.

The strong symbolism of the Hinomaru is said to represent the characteristics of the Japanese people and Japan's history: white is for peace and harmony; whilst red represents hardiness, bravery, strength and valour. The naval ensign is almost as recognisable as a symbol of Japan, and it is this flag that is represented by the reference to Japan as the "Land of the Rising Sun".

Top and bottom
Flag derived from the International maritime signal flag 'E' in use during the occupation of Japan, 1945-1952. Imperial Japanese Navy and Japanese Maritime Self-Defense Force ensign from 1889-1945, and from 1954-present.

NATIONAL FLAG STORIES
UNITED KINGDOM

The Three components of the Union Jack, also known as the Union Flag, are (from bottom to top) the Cross of St Andrew for Scotland, the Irish saltire of St Patrick and the Cross of St George for England.

The history of the British flag, the Union Jack, dates back to 1603 when James VI of Scotland inherited the English and Irish thrones, becoming James I and uniting the crowns of England, Scotland and Ireland. In 1606 a new flag was designed in order to symbolise this union. The red English cross—associated with St George was combined with the Scottish saltire of St Andrew to make the first Union Jack. Unhappy with the forefronting of the English symbol in this design, many Scots flew a variation of the flag for a time, in which the St Andrew's Cross was placed more prominently. It was not felt necessary to illustrate Wales in this flag; as it had been annexed by Edward I in 1282 and was thus felt to be implicitly represented by the Cross of St George.

Ireland was also unrepresented in the first Union Jack. During The Protectorate of 1658-1660, Cromwell decided to symbolise the country through the insertion of the Irish coat of arms, although after the Restoration this was eliminated in favour of the saltire of St Patrick.

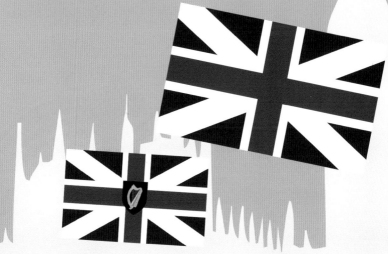

Left to right
Scottish Union Jack, 1606-1701.
Union Jack with Irish Coat of Arms, 1658-1660.
Union Jack, 1606-1801.

43

NATIONAL FLAG STORIES
UNITED STATES OF AMERICA

The flag of the United States of America–also known as "Old Glory"–is arguably the most recognisable flag in the world and is a symbol of national pride and strength in the US. The US national anthem, "The Star Spangled Banner", is a tribute to the flag and the freedom it is seen to represent.

There was no official flag of the US until the signing of the Declaration of Independence in 1776. However, the flags flown by the 13 states that fought the British in the Revolutionary War do have significant historical relevance. At the outbreak of the Revolutionary War, America was comprised of 13 British colonies. Although these colonies were officially under the jurisdiction of the British Parliament, its legitimacy was rejected by many of the colonists who believed that the lack of representation in the colonies constituted a violation of the Rights of Englishmen. The increasing dissatisfaction with the British led to the 13 states establishing the Second Continental Congress in 1775 and authorising the creation of a Continental Army.

Top to bottom
The Gadsden flag, c 1775.
The Culpeper Minutemen flag, c 1775.
Grand Union or Continental flag 1775.

British troops began to arrive on the east coast of America in retaliation and in 1776 it was declared that the Congress was in rebellion and acting as traitors to the Crown. The colonies responded by rejecting the British monarchy, claiming their own sovereignty as a single nation with the signing of the Declaration of Independence.

The 13 colonies that were initially represented in the United States of America were Virginia, New York, Massachusetts, New Hampshire, New Jersey, Maryland, Rhode Island, Connecticut, Delaware, North Carolina, South Carolina, Pennsylvania and Georgia. During the Revolutionary War the various groups fighting against the British had their own banners, although ironically many of these were similar in design to British flags. A banner flown at the battle of Bunker Hill for example features a St George's Cross in the canton, as well as a pine tree that was used in historical New England flags. Other flags of the revolution featured the defiant slogan "Don't tread on me", and variations of this can be seen on the flags of Gadsden, the Culpeper Minutemen and the First Navy Jack, still in use today.

Top to bottom
Bennington flag, 1777-1795.
"Betsy Ross" flag, 1777-1795.
American flag design depicting an additional star for the State of Michigan, in place from 1837-1845.

The banner of George Washington, the Grand Union flag, is regarded by many as the first flag of the United States, although interestingly this was actually the most British in style, featuring a Union Jack in the canton and strongly resembling the British East Indian Company flag.

It was decided that the flag of the new United States should feature 13 stripes to represent the colonies and 13 stars in the union to represent a new constellation– this is often referred to as the "Betsy Ross" flag. As more states were added to the Constitution, the number of stars in the canton grew, facilitating many design changes. Any updated designs incorporating additional states become official every 4 July on Independence Day. The most recent addition to the flag was Hawaii in 1960, bringing the number of stars to 50, representing the 50 US states. This is now the longest standing US flag design in history.

Top and bottom
American flag design depicting an additional star for the State of Iowa, in place from 1847-1848.
American flag design depicting an additional star for the State of Colorado, in place from 1877-1890.

TWENTIETH CENTURY FLAGS
THE HAMMER AND SICKLE

Detail of Lenin from a painting representing the October 1917 Revolution, and featuring a hammer and sickle flag.

The hammer and sickle were the key motifs on the official flag of the Soviet Union from 1923-1991, which also included a red star in the canton of the flag to represent the rule of the Communist Party.

This iconography has remained a recognisable symbol of communism and is still often appropriated by left-wing political groups and countries–such as China–still operating under communist rule.

Initially, during the early establishment of the Communist regime in the USSR, the Bolsheviks considered the possibility of adding a sword to the existing hammer and sickle, but the idea was dismissed by Lenin as being too visually aggressive. The hammer instead is representative of the proletariat workers of the USSR; the sickle of the agricultural workers; whilst the colour red symbolises the blood that has been spilled of the common people. The flag is one of the most effective in succinctly representing the ideological beliefs and aims of those that designed it.

The Worker and Collective Farm Woman statue by Vera Mukhina. The statue stands outside the Russian Exhibition building in Moscow.

SWASTIKA FLAGS

Top The flag of the Nazi Party.
Bottom The national German flag, 1871–1918, reinstated for a period by the Nazis.

After taking control of Germany on 30 January 1933, Hitler's Nazi Party quickly swapped the black, red, gold flag of the Weimar Republic and replaced it with two legal national flags: the old black, white, red imperial tricolore and the official Nazi Party swastika flag. One year after Hitler's official inauguration as Führer, the dual flag arrangement was scrapped and the Nazi Party flag also became the official national flag of Germany. The new flag was unveiled at the 1935 Nazi Party rally in Nuremberg.

For a period, the Nazis would 'sanctify' swastika flags by touching them with the *Blutfahne* (blood flag), the swastika flag that was used by Hitler and early Nazis at their failed 1923 attempt to seize power by force at the Bier Hall Putsch.

The swastika was originally a symbol of Buddhism, Hinduism and Jainism; in ancient Sanskrit "svastika" means a lucky charm or auspicious object. Although the Nazis inverted the direction of the symbol, the image of the swastika in many peoples minds remains synonymous with the Nazi regime and their reign of terror. In many Western countries, and particularly in Germany, displaying the Nazi swastika is now illegal.

Above The flag of the Finnish Training Air Wing with two swastikas, and a third atop the flag pole, 1918-present.
Below The Jain, an Asian five coloured flag.

ICONIC FLAG MOMENTS IN HISTORY

American soldiers raised the US flag atop Mount Suribachi during the Battle of Iwo Jima to signify their victory over the Japanese. This now legendary image, captured by Joe Rosenthal, has come to represent the American triumph over the Japanese in August 1945 and the subsequent end of the Second World War and America's rise as a super power.

During the latter days of the Battle of Berlin, the Soviets–who had nearly taken complete control of the city–famously raised the flag of the USSR atop the Reichstag, the parliament building of the German Empire. As iconic as this image became, it was actually a reconstruction of an earlier event that had not been documented. The photographer, Yeugeny Khaldei, altered the image by adding more smoke in the background to make for a more dramatic scene. He also removed a second watch from the arm of a soldier, which could have implied that he had looted one of them.

FLYING THE FLAG ON THE MOON

At 2:56 (UTC) on 21 July, 1969, Neil Armstrong made his famous "one small step for man, one giant leap for mankind" speech. Further to that, he celebrated his victory by planting the flag of the United States on the Moon's surface before the incredulous eyes of the world. The planting of the flag was actually far more tricky than first meets the eye. For starters, NASA had to pass a United Nations treaty that bans the national appropriation of outer space, or any celestial territory, which the flag could have implied. There was also the problem of how to store the flag on the lunar module to protect it on the journey up, as space was so limited in the craft. A young designer at the Johnson Space Center was entrusted with the task of resolving this, and he came up with a telescoping horizontal rod, sewn into a seam on the top of the flag, which could be extended out. Armstrong later recounted the troubling vicissitudes that accompanied the historical planting of the flag: "As hard as we tried, the telescope wouldn't fully extend. Thus the flag which should have been flat had it's own permanent wave." This explanation has been given as the justification for the apparent movement of the flag in imagery of the lunar landings, which many people believe provides proof for the whole event being a hoax as the lack of gravity on the Moon would mean that the flag should have remained static.

FLAG FAMILIES

Turkey

Cuba

Italy

Georgia

Flag of the
Arab Revolt

Congo

When one looks at world flags it becomes apparent that while each country flies its own, there are some underlying similarities, design cross-overs, and colours or elements that recur in some form or other between different national flags. The most ubiquitous similarities are defined as Flag Families. A single flag can belong to one or more Families; for example, some may display the Pan-Arab colours as well as the Muslim Cross. In many cases these similarities have a historical or political significance and may indicate a shared history or cultural kinship.

THE CHRISTIAN CROSS

The cross is an ancient symbol, which was employed by peoples in Mesopotamia, Scandinavia, China and Greece; today, its main association lies with Christianity, however. The Jerusalem Flag is one of the oldest examples of the cross being employed on a flag. This flag displayed five golden crosses on a white background. Denmark was the first nation to shift the position from the centre of the field as it had always been employed, to one side. Sweden, 1569, Norway, 1821, Iceland, 1919, and others later followed this example in their own flags. The Maltese Cross is a more elaborate variation on the Christian Cross, employed in 1561. Current nations within this family include Denmark, Switzerland and Sweden.

Brazil, Naval Jack

Denmark

England

Finland

Georgia

Greece

Dominican Republic

Iceland

Malta, Civic Ensign of

Norway

Kingdom of Jerusalem

Québec

Sweden

Switzerland

Algeria

Dagestan
(1919-1920)

Egypt (1952)

Maldives

Libya (1951)

Mauritania

Tunisia

Turkey

Pakistan

South Arabia
Federation

THE MUSLIM CRESCENT

Of all the symbols that have illustrated the history of humanity, the crescent is one of the most ancient. Inscribed as early as 2300 BC on Akkadian seals, the crescent was later adopted by the Mesopotamians and Phoenicians, reaching as far as Carthage in Tunisia. The Turks adopted it in their own iconography in the twelfth century, making it the main symbol of Islam since. The Muslim crescent is often accompanied by a star. Contemporary nations that display this symbol on their flags include Azerbaijan, Brunei, Comoros, Malasya, Maldives, Mauritania, Northern Cyprus, Pakistan, Singapore, Tunisia, Turkmenistan, Uzbekistan and Western Sahara.

France

Bolivia

Bulgaria

Chad

Gabon

Germany

Guinea

Hungary

Italy

Lithuania

Romania

THE TRICOLORE

On the eve of the French Revolution in 1789, the Paris militia were given blue and red cockades, with the Marquis de Lafayette offering a similar cockade to King Louis XVI later that year, who added to it the royal white one. The leaders of the revolution and the people of Paris consequently employed these colours as the "colours of liberty", with the Constituent Assembly approving the new French *drapeau* *tricolore* on 24 October 1790. The French Tricolore, and vertical alignment of three colours in general, became the symbol of the Republican Movement internationally. Contemporary tricolore flags include those of Andorra, Belgium, Cameroon, Chad, Guinea, Ireland, Italy, Ivory Coast, Mali, Mexico, Moldova, Romania, Rwanda and Senegal.

THE STARS AND STRIPES

The first and most famous stars and stripes appear on the American flag. This flag has undergone both minor and major changes throughout its history. In 1815 the Hawaiian King devised a way to incorporate the tricolore stripes of the American flag and the British Union Jack in the Hawaiian flag, to combine the symbols of the most influential powers in the Pacific into the flag of Hawaii. The stars and stripes have since come to stand for the ideals of liberty and democracy. Other countries that have since adopted the stars and stripes have been Argentina, Chile, Cuba, Greece, Liberia, Malaysia, Puerto Rico, Togo, and Uruguay, amongst many others.

Arizona

Catalonia

Cuba

European Union

Liberia

Louisiana (1861–1962)

Madrid, State of

Morocco

Panama

Hawaii (1815–1825)

Somalia

United States

Uruguay

Vietnam

Washington, DC

Algeria

Egypt (1952)

Iraq

Jordan

Palestine

Somaliland

Sudan

Syria

United Arab
Emirates

Western Sahara

THE PAN-ARAB COLOURS

The emergence of the Pan-Arab colours can be traced back to the history of the Arab Revolt. In 1914 the central committee of the Young Arab Society in Beirut professed that the liberated Arab independent state should be represented by white, standing for the Umayyad dynasty; black for the colour of the Abbasids; and green–the symbolic colour of Islam and the Fatimid dynasty of caliphs. The Pan-Arab colours were officially born on 10 June 1916, the day of the Arab Revolt. The revolution in Egypt that overthrew the monarchy in 1952, introduced the Arab Liberation Flag with the Pan-Arab colours.

Kuwait

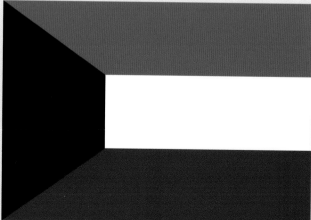

THE PAN-AFRICAN COLOURS

Ethiopia is the oldest independent state of Africa. Consequently, its green, yellow, and red flag was an inspiration for all future African states, along with the red, black and green flag of Marcus Garvey, created for the Universal Negro Improvement Association. Ghana was the first to include the colours of Ethiopia, together with the black star of Garvey's flag. Many countries have since followed this trend, forming the family of Pan-African colours.

Ethiopia

Angola

Biafra

Central African Republic

Congo, Republic of the

Uganda

Ghana

Guinea Bissau

Guinea

Guyana

The flag of Marcus Garvey, Universal Negro Improvement Association

Mozambique

Sao Tome and Principe

South Africa

RELIGIOUS FLAGS
CHRISTIAN

Of all the major religions in the world, Christianity appears to have the most flags. These include flags representing different churches, such as the Greek Orthodox flag, the Church of Scotland's flag and the Coptic flag; and Christian city states, such as the Vatican. Even some individuals have their own flags, such as the Bishop of Canterbury. The Christian flag itself was designed in the early twentieth century to represent the Christian faith as a whole, but has been adopted mainly by Protestant churches in North America, Africa and Latin America.

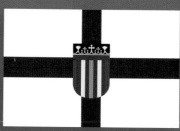

Top and bottom
Christian flag, early twentieth century–present.
Coptic flag, 2005–present.

Clockwise from top left
Greek Orthodox flag,
1000 AD-present.
Flag of the Vatican State,
1929-present.
Episcopal Church flag, ND.
Standard of the Church
of Scotland, 1560-present.

The Cross of St George depicts a red cross on a white background and is the traditional symbol of St George, patron saint of England. For this reason, it is fitting that it should appear on both the flags of England and of the City of London, alongside being adopted by other countries and regions including Georgia and the historic Kingdom of Asturias. St George's Cross should not be confused with the Swiss Cross, as in contrast to the latter, its arms reach all the way to the edges of the flag.

Clockwise from top left
Flag of the City of London, ND.
Flag of England, 1348-present.
Ceremonial flag of Greece, 1828-present.
Flag of the City of Nanaimo in British
Columbia, Canada, ND.
Flag of Canada, 1921-1957.
Flag of New South Wales,
Australia, 1876-present.
Flag of the Kingdom of Asturias, ND.
Flag of Georgia, 2004-present.

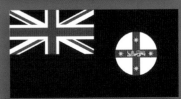

BUDDHIST

Buddhist
Prayer flags.

International
Buddhist flag.

Buddhist flag
of Thailand.

The Buddhist flag was designed in the nineteenth century, and although some countries display their own versions, such as Thailand, this one is recognised internationally. The blue (*Nila*) stands for loving, kindness, peace and universal compassion; yellow (*Pita*) represents the middle path, emptiness and balance; red (*Lohita*) the blessings of practice, achievement, wisdom, virtue, fortune and dignity; white (*Odata*) stands for the purity of Dharma, leading to liberation, outside of time or space; and orange (*Manjesta*) represents Buddha's teachings and wisdom.

Buddhist Prayer Flags, often seen in the Himalayas, are rectangular cloths of different colours strung together as a blessing, as well as to evoke peace, compassion, strength, and wisdom. Traditionally they display texts and images printed in woodblock.

HINDU

The most common Hindu flag is a triangular red or saffron flag. Many deities also have their own flags, flown on top of temples or in front of homes, standing alone or displayed together.

SIKH

The Sikh flag displays the Khanda, a major symbol of Sikhism, which represents "God's universal and creative power".

PROTEST FLAGS

Flags have a potent role in protests
of different kinds and express, for
example, cultural pride and heritage
or political aims and aspirations.

SAVE

1 Flag of Anarcha-feminism. 2 The American flag
upside down should only be displayed as a sign
of distress or danger, otherwise it is understood
as a sign of disrespect and protest. 3 Anarcho-
syndicalism or Anarcho-Communist flag.
4 Anarcho-green flag. 5 *African-American flag* by
artist David Hammonds, incorporating the colours
of the Universal Negro Improvement Association in
the US national flag design.

THE WHALES

4

5

MINORITY FLAGS

Flags are powerful tools in reflecting and fostering communal identities, and, as such, minorities often use them in order to enforce their cause. Some minority flags denote particular ethnicities, such as the Batwa flag, the Aboriginal People's flag of Australia, and

1 Batwa flag. 2 Aboriginal People's flag of Australia. 3 Ikurrina flag (official flag of the Basque Country Autonomous Community of Spain). 4 Corsican flag. 5 Arrano Beltza Basque Separatist flag. 6 Gay Pride flag. 7 Tibetan flag. 8 Romany Gypsy flag. 9 Flag of Kurdistan.

the Romany Gypsy flag. Others represent minorities within existing States and voice a group's desire for autonomy or outright independence, such as in the case of Tibet, the Basque Country, Corsica and Kurdistan. Others, such as the Gay Pride flag have to do with sexual orientation. Overall minority flags operate on two levels, on the one hand they unite the members of a particular group; and on the other they communicate to the rest of the world a groups' desire for recognition and respect.

TRADE UNION BANNERS

National Union of Mineworkers — Yorkshire Area

Come Dungeons Dark or Gallows Grim

Stillingfleet Branch

Proud symbols of protest flags are a common sight in trade union demonstrations. Each union has their own 'flag', or banner, expressive of the movement's identity and aspirations.

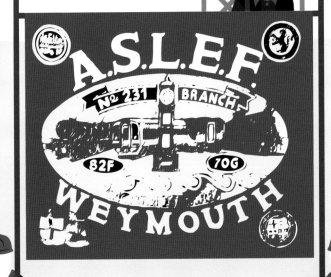

THE RED FLAG

The symbolism of the red flag is closely associated with socialism and left-wing politics. It first emerged as a symbol of the working class and was used as a tool for protest against right-wing politics during the Merthyr Rising in Wales in 1831. The red flag was also a prominent symbol in France during the Revolutions of 1848 and came to represent communism after it was adopted by the Paris Commune in 1871. The red flag represented the British Labour Party until the late 1980s—the song "The Red Flag" is still sung at the end of the Labour Party conference, as it is with the Irish Labour Party, who use the song as their national anthem. The Red Flag was written by Jim Connell, a migrant Irish worker in London, after attending a London Dock strike in 1889; he penned the lyrics on his train journey back from Charing Cross station to his home in Honor Oak, South London. It is likely that Connell's inspiration for the song came as he watched the train guard raise and lower his red signal flag on the platform. The song is normally sung to the tune of "O Tannenbaum". The song has in recent years been covered by contemporary political musician Billy Bragg, who set the lyrics to the tune of "The White Cockade", which is interestingly the original tune that Connell intended when writing the song.

THE PEOPLE'S FLAG IS DEEPEST RED,
IT SHROUDED OFT OUR MARTYRED DEAD,
AND ERE THEIR LIMBS GREW STIFF AND COLD,
THEIR HEARTS' BLOOD DYED ITS EVERY FOLD.
THEN RAISE THE SCARLET STANDARD HIGH.
WITHIN ITS SHADE WE LIVE AND DIE,
THOUGH COWARDS FLINCH AND TRAITORS SNEER,
WE'LL KEEP THE RED FLAG FLYING HERE.
LOOK ROUND, THE FRENCHMAN LOVES ITS BLAZE,
THE STURDY GERMAN CHANTS ITS PRAISE,
IN MOSCOW'S VAULTS ITS HYMNS WERE SUNG
CHICAGO SWELLS THE SURGING THRONG.
IT WAVED ABOVE OUR INFANT MIGHT,
WHEN ALL AHEAD SEEMED DARK AS NIGHT;
IT WITNESSED MANY A DEED AND VOW,
WE MUST NOT CHANGE ITS COLOUR NOW.
IT WELL RECALLS THE TRIUMPHS PAST,
IT GIVES THE HOPE OF PEACE AT LAST;
THE BANNER BRIGHT, THE SYMBOL PLAIN,
OF HUMAN RIGHT AND HUMAN GAIN.
IT SUITS TODAY THE WEAK AND BASE,
WHOSE MINDS ARE FIXED ON PELF AND PLACE
TO CRINGE BEFORE THE RICH MAN'S FROWN,
AND HAUL THE SACRED EMBLEM DOWN.
WITH HEAD UNCOVERED SWEAR WE ALL
TO BEAR IT ONWARD TILL WE FALL;
COME DUNGEONS DARK OR GALLOWS GRIM,
THIS SONG SHALL BE OUR PARTING HYMN

FLAG BURNING

Flag burning is an act of desecration with the intention of damaging or destroying a flag in public. Flags are often burned to make a political statement, such as the burning of a national flag. Law in some countries actually forbids the destruction of national flags, whereas in others it is accepted as part of one's right to free speech and expression of opinions. There are also countries which forbid the burning of their own national flag, but not the burning of other's. Burning the flag is not always an act of abuse, however; it can, in some countries—for example in the United States—mean a dignified retirement for a flag, which is no longer deemed suitable for display.

SURRENDER

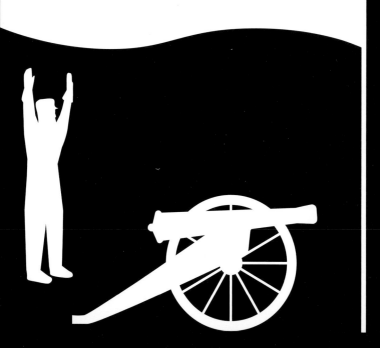

THE WHITE FLAG IS A UBIQUITOUS SYMBOL OF SURRENDER THAT CAN BE TRACED BACK TO ROMAN TIMES. IT IS INTERNATIONALLY RECOGNISED AS A SINCERE SIGN OF A DESIRE FOR TRUCE OR CEASEFIRE AND AS A PLEA FOR NEGOTIATION AND COMMUNICATION, AS STIPULATED IN THE GENEVA CONVENTION.

NO SURRENDER

AS A DIRECT CONTRAST, THE WAVING OF A BLACK FLAG SYMBOLISES A REFUSAL TO SURRENDER, AND WAS FIRST USED BY THE CONFEDERATE ARMY IN THE AMERICAN CIVIL WAR. HOWEVER, DURING THE SECOND WORLD WAR, THE NAZIS APPROPRIATED THE BLACK FLAG AS ONE OF SURRENDER, INSTRUCTING THEIR U-BOATS TO FLY IT WHEN GIVING THEMSELVES IN TO ALLIED PORTS.

BLACK FLAGS

A black flag can be seen as a refusal to represent and is therefore a fitting symbol for the anarchists' rejection of representative politics and nation-states. The black flag used by anarchists since the 1880s is used either in its plain form or decorated with the letter 'A' inside a circle. The symbol is believed to refer to Pierre-Joseph Proudhon's assertion that "anarchy is order".

In sixteenth century Europe, the revolting farmers used the black flag in the Peasant's War–or 'Bauernkrieg'–the largest popular uprising in Europe before the

French Revolution. Black Flag was also the name of an influential American hardcore punk band active in the 1970s and 1980s. Raymond Pettibon, a renowned artist, whose brother Greg Ginn was the guitarist and founder of Black Flag, designed the band's logo. Inspired by the Dutch Modernist movement de Stijl, the logo depicted an abstracted flag, made up of four vertical black bars, waving in the wind.

FLAG ETIQUETTE
FOLDING
OLD GLORY

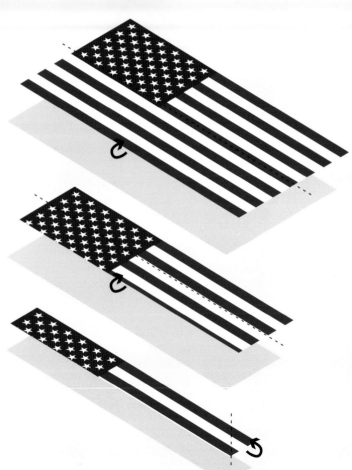

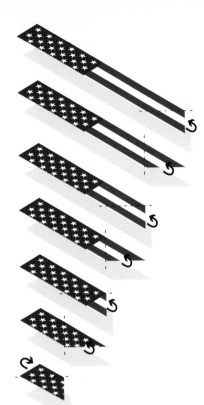

The United States of America flag, often referred to as "Old Glory", "Stars and Stripes" and "The Star Spangled Banner", is comprised of 50 stars and 13 stripes. Each star represents a state, with the stripes standing for the original colonies that rebelled against the British monarchy to become the first 13 states.

Although not mentioned in the official Flag Code, the military custom holds that "Old Glory" should be folded into a triangular shape so that the red and white are wrapped into the blue. Each fold is symbolic and their meanings are stated at the Flag Folding Ceremony recited during holidays including Memorial Day and Veterans Day.

FLAG ETIQUETTE
FOLDING THE UNION JACK

There is no specific procedure for folding the Union Jack. However, one way to fold it neatly, ready for its next use, is exemplified here.

FLAG ETIQUETTE
FOLDING BANDEIRA DE PORTUGAL

On a formal occasion four people fold the Portuguese flag, each folding one side to reveal a square shape, with only the Portuguese shield visible.

AMERICAN FLAG ETIQUETTE

The United States Flag Code sets out regulations for the display and care of the American flag. The code is US Federal Law but, as evident from countless Americans bedecked in "Stars and Stripes" regalia, failure to comply does not carry a penalty.

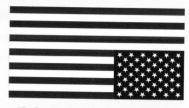

The flag should only be flown upside down as a distress signal.

The flag should not be flown in bad weather.

When a flag is damaged, it should be disposed of with dignity.

The flag should never be only partially illuminated.

A good American keeps his flag clean.

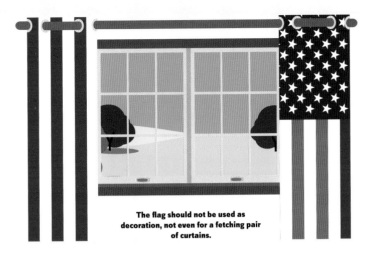

The flag should not be used as decoration, not even for a fetching pair of curtains.

When the flag is lowered, no part of it should touch the ground.

The flag should not be worn as clothing or as part of a costume.

The flag should not be printed on cushions, handkerchiefs, napkins–anything that will be disposed of after temporary use.

The flag should not be used for holding, carrying, or delivering anything.

THE PLEDGE OF ALLEGIANCE

The original "Pledge of Allegiance" was written by Francis Bellamy in 1892 and was published in a well-known children's magazine, *The Youth's Companion*. The Pledge was originally intended as an 'inoculation' to protect Americans and recent immigrants to the US from the 'virus' of radicalism and subversion.

According to the US Flag Code, the Pledge "should be rendered by standing at attention facing the flag with the right hand over the heart. When not in uniform men should remove any non-religious headdress with their right hand and hold it at the left shoulder, the hand being over the heart. Persons in uniform should remain silent, face the flag, and render the military salute."

I PLEDGE ALLEGIANCE TO THE FLAG OF THE UNITED STATES OF AMERICA, AND TO THE REPUBLIC FOR WHICH IT STANDS, ONE NATION UNDER GOD, INDIVISIBLE, WITH LIBERTY AND JUSTICE FOR ALL.

FLAGS AT HALF-MAST

Flying a flag at half-mast, or half-staff, signifies mourning and is used as a mark of respect for important figures that have passed away.

Many people believe that the practice of flying flags at half-mast began centuries ago when flags were lowered to allow space for the invisible flag of death to fly at the top of the mast–symbolising death's power, presence and prominence. In some countries, such as the UK, and in most military contexts, a half-mast flag is still flown exactly one width down from its normal position to allow for the 'flag of death'. In other countries and largely when there is a larger flag on a shorter hoist, a half-mast flag is flown halfway down the mast.

When hoisting a flag to half-mast it should be first hoisted to the finial for a moment, and then lowered to half-mast. The flag should be raised to the finial again before it is lowered for the day.

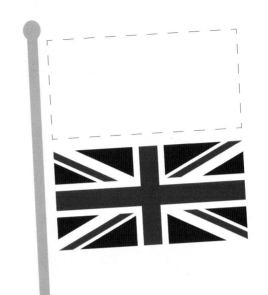

93

FLAGS AT SEA
INTERNATIONAL SIGNAL FLAGS AND PENNANTS

Alfa   Bravo   Charlie   Delta   Echo   Foxtrot

Golf   Hotel   India   Juliet   Kilo   Lima

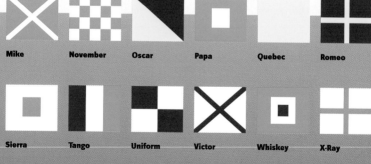

Mike   November   Oscar   Papa   Quebec   Romeo

Sierra   Tango   Uniform   Victor   Whiskey   X-Ray

Yankee   Zulu

These are often seen on boats and make up an important aspect of communication at sea. The signal flags can be used to spell out short messages, although more commonly they communicate special meanings by being displayed individually or in particular combinations.

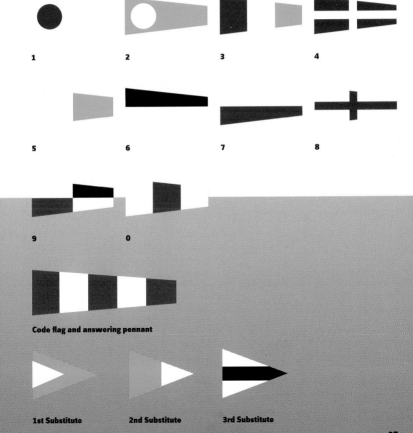

1

2

3

4

5

6

7

8

9

0

Code flag and answering pennant

1st Substitute

2nd Substitute

3rd Substitute

DRESSED OVERALL

Flags are used to dress ships for ceremonial occasions, either overall or at the masthead. The overall is used when the ship is harboured, while masthead flags are used on the way into, or within the vicinity of a harbour. Yachts dressed in their overalls for a regatta are a spectacle to see.

HOMEWARD-BOUND PENNANT AND PAYING-OFF PENNANT

A homeward-bound pennant is also known as a commission pennant or paying-off pennant. It is usually at least the length of its ship and can extend up to 73.9 metres (80 yards) on top of a normal pennant. It used to be a widespread custom on a ship returning home after a prolonged period of military service to wear a homeward-bound pennant as it entered back into its home port. The term 'paying-off pennant' derives from the fact that sailors were usually only paid once they returned home after overseas service, a practice used in order to avoid desertion.

In the United States Navy it is customary for homeward-bound pennants to measure one foot for each member of the ship's crew on service abroad for more than nine months. Contrary to the paying off pennant, the US homeward-bound pennant should never exceed the length of the ship itself.

= 1 ft

SEMAPHORE FLAGS

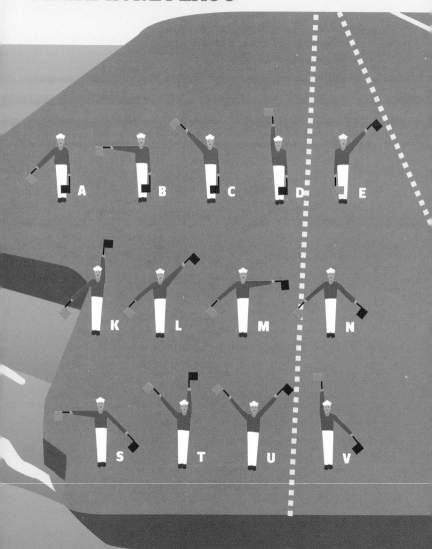

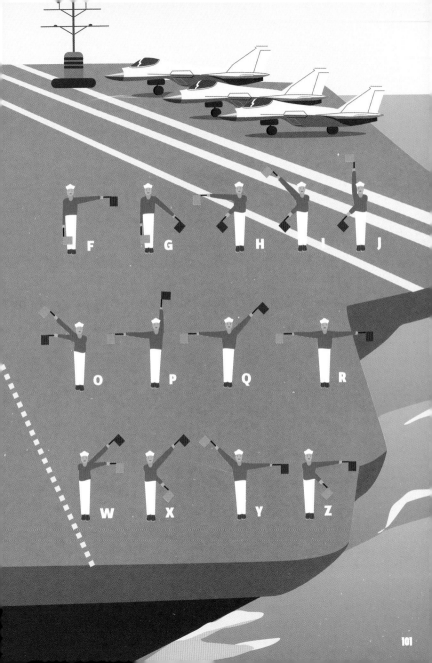

PIRATE FLAGS

EMANUEL WYNNE

The first record of a pirate flying the infamous Jolly Roger mentions the French pirate Emanuel Wynne. Wynne began his career by terrorising the coasts of Carolina, later moving to the Caribbean, where he was able to amass copious booty. The hourglass depicted on his flag is a common pirate symbol, together with the skull and crossbones, and is a warning to the pirate's victims that their time is running out.

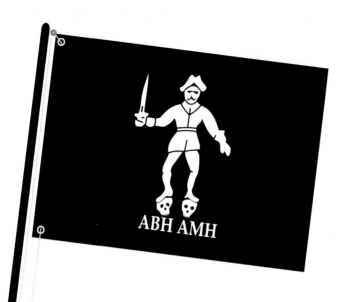

ABH AMH

BARTHOLOMEW ROBERTS

Arguably the most successful pirate of the Golden Age of Piracy, Bartholomew Roberts, born John Roberts, 1682-1722, is rumoured to have seized 470 ships in the Caribbean and off the coasts of Africa and Canada. Roberts is also one of four pirate captains mentioned in Robert Louis Stevenson's *Treasure Island*.

Initially a Welsh sailor, Roberts was forced into piracy at the age of 37, after being captured by Howell Davis. When, just a month after his capture, Davis was killed at Principe Island, Roberts was elected captain of *The Rover*. Roberts was killed in battle four years later.

CHRISTOPHER MOODY

Christopher Moody's life remains a mystery; he may have been part of Bartholomew Roberts' crew for some time, but then pirated independently off the coast of North and South Carolina between 1713 and 1718. He met his end when he was captured and hung at Cape Coast Castle in Cabo Corso, Ghana, and is remembered for his distinctive flag, in which the red background symbolising blood signalled his ruthless intents to his victims.

BLACK BEARD

Edward Teach, 1680-1718, otherwise known as the infamous Blackbeard, was a British pirate who terrorised ships off the coasts of America. He began pirating in 1716 when he joined Benjamin Hornigold's crew but was soon commanding his own ship, the *Queen Anne's Revenge*. His career as a pirate ended when he was killed in a battle against a force of sailors led by Lieutenant Robert Maynard.

SUBMARINE JOLLY ROGER

The first use of a Jolly Roger as a victory flag on a submarine has been attributed to Commanding Office Max Horton, of the British vessel *HMS E9*, during the First World War. The flag was flown as the submarine entered port in September 1914 after torpedoing the German cruiser *HMS Hela*. The use of the Jolly Roger in this context was an irreverent reference to a statement made by Admiral Sir Arthur Wilson–former Controller of the Royal Navy–who had infamously stated that the introduction of submarines to rival navies was "underhand, unfair and damned un-English"; he would convince the British Admiralty to hang any captured enemy crews as pirates.

Numerous submarines continued this tradition by designing their own Jolly Roger flag, with each element a reference to a particular victory or feat.

The Jolly Roger of the Tradewind submarine.

The Jolly Roger of the Shakespeare submarine.

Japanese Merchant Ship torpedoed

Warship torpedoed

Merchant Ship torpedoed

U-boat sunk by torpedo

Vesssel damaged but not sunk

Small vessels sunk by gunfire

Supply trips to under seige Malta

Aircraft shot down

Train or track destroyed by gunfire

Ship sunk by demolition charges

Gun action

Very small vessel sunk

Marking operations for amphibious landings

Marking operations for amphibious landings

Minelaying operations

Air or sea rescue

Chariot recovery operation

Cloak and dagger operations

Submarine went below safe diving depth

A ramming!

1 **Yellow and red striped flag:** this flag communicates to the drivers that the track has been rendered slippery, usually by oil or water.

2 **Black with orange circle flag:** this will be accompanied by a car number and warns the driver that his car has a mechanical problem that warrants returning to the pit.

3 **Half black, half white flag:** this will also be accompanied by a car number and signals unsporting behaviour. If the driver does not respond to this warning by rectifying his behaviour, a black flag will ensue.

4 **Red flag:** placed at the start line. When waved, it terminates the race or the practice session. Red flags positioned at each observer's post around the circuit will also be waved, simultaneously. The red flag is usually used in the case of a serious accident or when poor track conditions force racers to interrupt the race.

5 **Black flag:** accompanied by a car number, this flag orders the car to return to its pit and often signals to the driver that his race finishes here.

6 **White flag:** warns the driver that there is a slow moving vehicle ahead.

7 Yellow flag: the yellow flag indicates danger, such as a stranded car ahead on the tracks. If a single yellow flag is waved, cars have to slow down. When two yellow flags are waved simultaneously, the drivers have to slow down considerably and be ready to stop. Overtaking is prohibited.

8 Blue flag: this flag indicates to a driver that he is about to be lapped and that he should enable the faster car to overtake. If the driver passes three blue flags and still does not allow his opponent to overtake, he may be penalised.

9 Green flag: when a driver sees the green flag he knows that the danger alert previously indicated by the yellow flag has been lifted.

10 Black and white chequered flag: waving the chequered flag determines the end of the race at the allotted time. It is waved when the first car to reach the finish line arrives and is shown to each successive car that crosses the line after this.

10

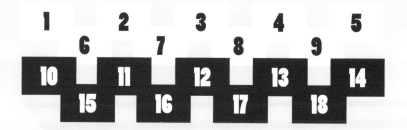

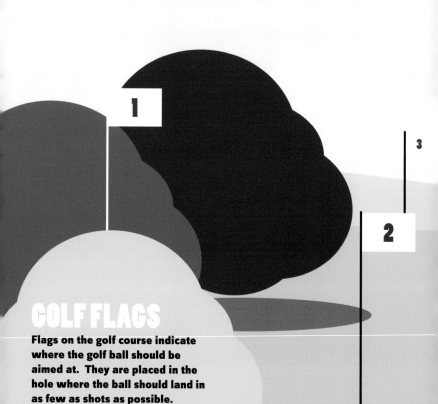

GOLF FLAGS

Flags on the golf course indicate where the golf ball should be aimed at. They are placed in the hole where the ball should land in as few as shots as possible.

When planning a stroke it is useful to consider whether there are any obstacles between your ball and the flag. When standing at a dogleg angle to the flag, it may be a better idea to shoot the ball to a better location. In the case of short holes, beware of nearby greenside hazards such as water areas or sand traps.

Flags in golf are also helpful to assess the direction and the strength of the wind. Being able to tell where the wind is blowing from is an advantage when planning a shot.

When making a shot into the green, flags help to judge the location of the hole. Flags are often colour-coded according to their location and whether they are in the middle, front or back of the green.

PITCH SPORT FLAGS

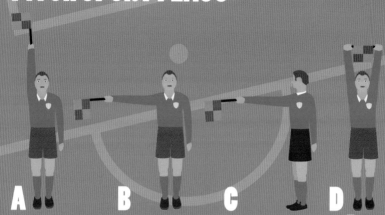

A   B   C   D

FOOTBALL

In football the referee and their assistants communicate with the aid of a flag. Here are some examples of uses of the flag in football.

A: Holding the flag towards the sky is a sign for the referee to blow the whistle and pause the game.

B: When the ball is out of bounds the assistant raises the flag and the game is paused. To continue the game the assistant positions the flag at a 45-degree angle, horizontally along the touch line. The game carries on with the team attacking in the direction of the flag taking the throw in.

C: In the case of a player being offside, the flag is pointed towards the offside and where the ball is to be placed for a free kick. Waving the flag back instead means that there is no advantage and the game continues once the flag is lowered. If the flag is held up at a 45-degrees it means the offside occurred on the far side of the field. Held down at 45-degrees, the flag indicates that the offside happened on the near side of the field in relation to the assistant. If officials hold the flag straight in front of them, the offside has occurred in the middle of the field.

D: A flag held above the head with both hands means that a substitution is taking place and the game is paused to allow for this.

AMERICAN FOOTBALL

Penalty flag: yellow cloths are used to mark the location of penalties or infractions occurring during a match. These are usually wrapped around a weight, such as sand beans, so that it can be accurately thrown to the target. Flags also indicate fouls, but if officials run out of flags and see multiple infractions, they may drop their hat on the floor instead.

Red flag; Coach's Challenge: originally, coaches could challenge play by using a pager to buzz the referee with the red flag as a backup, but the penalty flag system was far more popular with the coaches.

29/05/1921
United
Kingdom

23/03/1953
Switzerland

25/05/1960
China

01/05/1963
United States

22/05/1965
India

14/10/1978
Germany

13/05/1979
Yugoslavia

13/02/1980
Poland

14/05/1980
Spain

04/05/1982
Soviet Union

11/05/1970
Japan

05/05/1973
Italy

15/09/1977
South Korea

03/05/1978
Austria

14/10/1978
France

05/10/1982
Canada

20/04/1984
Bulgaria

03/10/1984
Australia

04/10/1984
Netherlands

15/10/1984
Slovakia

POPULAR CULTURE

The ubiquitous nature of flags, as well as their iconic power, explains why they pervade popular culture, history, politics and geography.

The Union Jack was a symbol for the UK punk rock scene in the late 1970s and early 1980s—the Sex Pistols in particular used the symbolism of the flag to denounce the Monarchy and the Conservative Government. Through the use of the flag by such bands, the Union Jack actually became a symbol of unconventional patriotism for the punk generation and a fashionable symbol of the day.

The relevance of the "Stars and Stripes" in popular culture has meant that the flag of the United States is also a frequently used symbol in fashion such as on shoes, t-shirts and jeans. There is no limit to the different flags that can be employed in culture and the ways in which they can be appropriated, as these colourful fingernails clearly testify.

It is not hard to imagine why art has often illustrated, appropriated and commented on flags throughout history. In Eugène Delacroix's *Liberty Leading the People*, the newly designed drapeau tricolore–symbolic of the revolution, as well as Republican ideals as a whole–is being waved triumphantly by the allegory of Liberty, who guides the people into the revolution. Artists have also used flags in other, sometimes more critical, ways. Pop Art in particular has often explored the aesthetic and representational possibilities offered by flags, such as in Jasper Johns' *Three Flags*, and Roy Lichtenstein's *Forms in Space*. By altering national flags in his *Album le Rouge* by having

red paint ooze, smudge and drip from them, the French artist Gérard Fromanger delivers quite a bold statement about the bloody history of contemporary nations. More recently new generations of artists, working in various media have continued to play with the language of flags in critical ways, as does the British graffiti artist, Banksy, who's evocation of the flag through a plastic Tesco bag, shrewdly expresses darker concerns about the role of consumerism in contemporary society.

Above Gérard Fromanger, *Album Le Rouge*, 1970.
Opposite Eugène Delacroix, *Liberty Leading the People*, 1830.

Banksy.

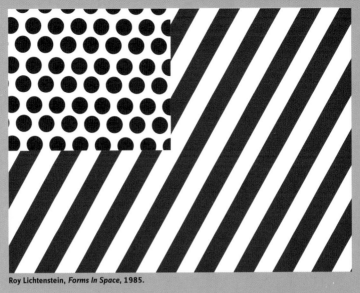

Roy Lichtenstein, *Forms In Space*, 1985.

Jasper Johns, *Three Flags*, 1958.

FICTIONAL FLAGS

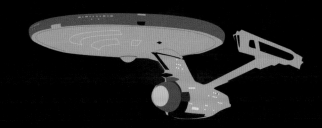

Tintin

1984

Monty Python and the Holy Grail

The Lord of the Rings

Barbar

Fictional flags are often as well known as genuine ones. The presence of flags within stories, especially visually in films and television programmes, helps us to suspend our disbelief and believe that the worlds that are being presented to us have as rich a history as our own. Flags within fantasy sagas such as *The Lord of the Rings* create a sense of a densely populated and diverse Middle Earth; in science fiction, in stories such as *Star Trek* flags enforce the idea of a land that exists away from our own planet; and in dystopian future tales such as George Orwell's *1984* they project a believable and feared future that still seems connected to our present.

The Beatles: Help!

Star Wars

The Handmaid's Tale

Star Trek

The Simpsons

The Rocky Horror Picture Show

The Lord of the Rings

Ku Klux Klan

Italian National
Fascist Party

International
Satanic Pride

White Supremacy/
Confederate Battle

Al-Qaeda

BANNED/CULT FLAGS

Many flags representing racist or nefarious political and social movements have been banned from being flown, or have become loaded symbols of subversive intent. Fascist symbols such as the Nazi swastika flag, the flag of the Scutzstaffel (SS) and the Italian National Fascist Party flag have been banned by law in their countries of origin, as well as in other European states.

Other flags representing racist or fundamentalist movements such as those of the Klu Klux Klan, the former Confederate army and Al-Qaeda have a negative cult status.

Schutzstaffel

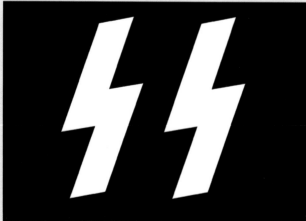

INTERNATIONAL FLAGS

Myriad flags have been designed to represent international unions and organisations. Flags created for continental associations of countries–such as the European Union–and political coalition–such as NATO and the United Nations–establish a sense of communal representation that transcends national borders. Some, such as those of the International Red Cross have gained an international ubiquity for their humanitarian connotations. Others simply represent international groups with particular niche interests.

United Nations

Organisation of the Petroleum Exporting Countries (OPEC)

Association of South East Asian Nations

International Federation of Vexillological Associations

European Union

Commonwealth

NATO

International Red Crescent

International Red Cross

International Red Crystal

Olympic flag

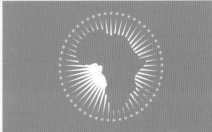

African Union

THE BIGGEST FLAG

202m/663ft

THE SMALLEST FLAG

The biggest flag the Guinness World Records has recorded to date is the Lebanese flag, revealed in October 2010 to celebrate the Lebanese Army's 65th anniversary. The flag measures a total of 65,650 square meters, beating the previous record holder Morocco, which was known to have covered a surface of 60,000 square metres. The cedar in the middle, which measures 10,452 square metres, actually refers to the country's total wooded area of 10,452 square kilometres. It was presented at the Lebanese Air Force Base in Rayak, Bekaa Valley, Lebanon.

The smallest flag to have been produced is believed to be a flag of Turkey measuring 700 nanometres wide. To put this into perspective, a human hair is usually around 50,000 nanometres in diameter. This flag was developed at the Bilknet University Nanophysics Department.

SOVEREIGN STATES

To date, there are 194 sovereign states in the world, consisting of all member states of the United Nations and Vatican City. A sovereign state can be classified as a defined territory; independent from other states and powers, that has its own government system and a permanent population. Each sovereign state has its own flag.

The flags featured on the following pages include the flags of each of the 50 states of the United States of America; Canada and its 15 provincial and official flags; and Brazil with its 27 state flags. Each flag is depicted with the flagpole to the left, with the exception of Iran and Iraq, where the flagpole is positioned to the right.

Afghanistan

Albania

Algeria

Andorra

Antigua and
Barbuda

Angola

Argentina

Armenia

Australia

Austria

Azerbaijan

Bahamas

Bahrain

Bangladesh

Barbados

Belarus

Belgium

Belize

Benin

Bhutan

Bolivia
(Plurinational
State of)

Bosnia and
Herzegovina

Botswana

Brazil (and the 27
state flags)

Acre

Alagoas

Amapá

Amazonas

Bahia

Ceara

Distrito Federal

Espírito Santo

Goiás

Maranhão

Mato Grosso

Mato Grosso do Sul

Minas Gerais

Paraíba

Paraná

Pará

Pernambuco

Piauí

Rio Grande do Norte

Rio de Janeiro

Rio Grande do Sul

Rondônia

Roraima

Santa Catarina

São Paulo

Sergipe

Tocantins

Brunei Darussalam

Bulgaria

Burkina Faso

Burundi

Cambodia

Cameroon

Canada (and the 15 provincial and official flags)

Alberta

British Columbia

Cape Breton Island

Labrador

Manitoba

New Bunswick

Newfoundland and Labrador

Northwest Territories

Nova Scotia

Nunavut

Ontario

Prince Edward Island

Québec

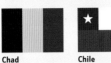

Saskatchewan

Yukon Territory

Cape Verde

Central African Republic

Chad

Chile

China

Colombia

Comoros

Congo (Democratic Republic of the)

Congo (Republic of the)

Costa Rica

Côte d'Ivoire

Croatia

Cuba

Cyprus

Czech Republic

Denmark

Djibouti

Dominica

Dominican Republic

East Timor

Ecuador

Egypt

El Salvador

Equatorial Guinea

Eritrea

Estonia

Ethiopia

Fiji

Finland

France

Gabon

Gambia

Georgia

Germany

Ghana

Greece

Grenada

Guatemala

Guinea Bissau

Guinea

Guyana

Haiti

Honduras

Hungary

Iceland

India

Indonesia

Iran (Islamic Republic of)

Iraq

Ireland

Israel

Italy

Jamaica

Japan

Jordan

Kazakhstan

Kenya

Kiribati

Korea (Democratic People's Republic of)

Korea (Republic of)

Kuwait

Kyrgyzstan

Lao People's Democratic Republic

Latvia

Lebanon

Lesotho

Liberia

Libya Arab Jamahiriya

Liechtenstein

Lithuania

Luxembourg

Macedonia (The Former Yugoslav Republic of)

Madagascar

Malawi

Malaysia

Maldives

Mali

Malta

Marshall Islands

Mauritania

Mauritus

Mexico

Micronesia (Federated States of)

Moldova (Republic of)

Monaco

Mongolia

Montenegro

Morocco

Mozambique

Myanmar

Namibia

Nauru

Nepal

Netherlands

New Zealand

Nicaragua

Niger

Nigeria

Norway

Oman

Pakistan

Palau

Panama

Papua New Guinea

Paraguay

Peru

Philippines

Poland

Portugal

Qatar

Romania

Russian Federation

Rwanda

Saint Kitts and Nevis

Saint Lucia

Saint Vincent and the Grenadines

Samoa

San Marino

Sao Tome and Principe

Saudi Arabia

Senegal

Serbia

Seychelles

Sierra Leone

Singapore

Slovakia

Slovenia

Solomon Islands

Somalia

South Africa

Spain (and the 17 regional flags)

Andalusia

Aragón

Asturias

Baleares

The Basque Country (País Vasco)

Canary Islands (Islas Canarias)

Cantabria

Castilla-La-Mancha

Castilla Y León

Catalonia (Catalunya)

Extremadura

Murcia

Galicia

La Rioja

Madrid

Navarre

Valencia

Sri Lanka

Sudan

Suriname

Swaziland

Sweden

Switzerland

Syrian Arab Republic

Tajikistan

Tanzania (United Republic of)

Thailand

Togo

Tonga

Trinidad and Tobago

Tunisia

Turkey

Turkmenistan

Tuvalu

Uganda

Ukraine

United Arab Emirates

United Kingdom

United States of America (and the 50 states)

Alabama

Alaska

Arizona

Arkansas

California

Colorado

Connecticut

Delaware

Florida

Georgia

Hawaii

Idaho

Illinois

Indiana

Iowa

Kansas

Kentucky

Louisiana

Maine

Maryland

Massachusetts

Michigan

Minnesota

Mississippi

Missouri

Montana

Nebraska

Nevada

New Hampshire

New Jersey

New Mexico

New York

North Carolina

North Dakota

Ohio

Oklahoma

Oregon

Oregon (reverse)

Pennsylvania

Rhode Island

South Carolina

South Dakota

Tennessee

Texas

Utah

Vermont

Virginia

Washington

West Virginia

Wisconsin

Wyoming

Uruguay

Uzbekistan

Vanuatu

Vatican City

Venezuela
(Bolivarian
Republic of)

Viet Nam

Yemen

Zambia

Zimbabwe

FLAG TERMS

BADGE
Typically a heraldic emblem which is added to an existing flag, of which popular imagery includes lions, eagles, horses and roses.

BREAK OUT
The unfurling of a flag that has been rolled in such a way that a sharp pull on the halyard will allow it to open out.

BUNTING
Decorative flags that are used as decoration for parades, celebrations etc., typically made of a durable material and woven together in a line.

BANNEROL
A small flag, often square, used at funerals and displaying the coat of arms of the deceased person—now obsolete.

BICOLOUR
A diagonally, horizontally or vertically divided flag featuring two colours and two equal sections.

CANTON
The upper hoist corner of a flag, or a rectangular field within this area.

COLOUR
Flag of military unit, usually referring to regimental colours.

COLOURS
A figurative term referring to any flag, particularly military and maritime flags.

COURTESY FLAG
A national flag flown by a foreign ship visiting that country.

DIPPING
The brief lowering of a flag as a sign of respect or deference.

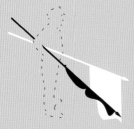

DRUM-BANNER
A small flag used to adorn a military parade drum.

ENSIGN
Maritime national flags flown from the stern of a boat.

EX-VOTO
A votive flag shown to fulfil a religious vow.

FERRULE
A metal ring atop a flagstaff, below the finial.

FINIAL
An ornamental design atop a flagstaff, often featuring crests, spearheads or animals.

FLAG
"A piece of stuff (usually bunting), varying in size, colour, and device, but usu. oblong or square, attached by one edge to a staff or to a halyard, used as a standard, ensign, or signal, and also for display."
Oxford Dictionary definition.

FLUTTER FLAG
A banner made from lightweight material, attached to a pole, often used for advertising. Also known as "Feather Flags".

139

FRINGE

The decorated edging of a flag, often comprising twisted thread or metal and used at parades and celebrations.

GONFANON

A pre-heraldic war flag with squared tails attached to a lance.

GUIDON

A long flag that tapers off into two rounded tails. It is often used for marking or signalling.

GUMPHION

A small funeral flag.

GARRISON

The largest US flag flown from military posts on special flag flying days.

MERCHANT FLAG

A national flag flown by commercial and privately owned vessels.

GONFALON

A flag hung from a crossbar and usually ending in tails. It is characteristic of Italy and Western Europe.

NAVAL ENSIGN/WAR ENSIGN

A national flag flown by naval vessels.

PARLEY FLAG

A white flag flown during war to request negotiations.

PAVILION

A highly stylised draped flag, typically red or blue and lined with ermine fur, onto which a coat of arms is depicted.

PILOT FLAG

A flag displayed by a vessel to signal the presence of a pilot onboard.

PRAYER FLAG

A small, colourful flag, used to express a prayer or blessing and often strung as bunting. Typical to Buddhism, these flags are traditionally woodblock printed, combining both texts and images.

PULLDOWN

A flag or bunting used to decorate a building.

RANK FLAG

Used to signify the civil or military status of an individual.

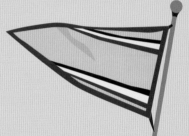

ROYAL STANDARD

A rank flag or banner bearing the royal coat of arms, flown in the presence of a monarch.

SIGNAL FLAG

Designed to communicate messages visually, signal flags often follow recognised designs, such as the International Code of Signals, and are often used at sea.

STREAMER

A long, narrow flag or banner, often used for decoration.

SWALLOWTAILED

A triangular section cut out from the fly end of a flag, historically typical of pennants of Northern Europe.

TYPE FLAG

A prototype flag from which subsequent flags are made, of which the specification of pattern and colour is often regulated by law.

UNIQUE FLAG

A flag of singular design intended for one use only.

VANE

A small metal flag placed on the top of buildings, otherwise known as a weather vane.

VEXILLARY

The bearer of an ensign or standard.

VEXILLIUM

A Roman cavalry flag.

VEXILLOID

An object replacing the function of a flag. It often consists of a staff topped with an emblem, such as a carved animal.

WAFT

A flag that has been tied in a knot to signal distress–used at sea but now obsolete.

WAR FLAG

A national flag flown over a military base.

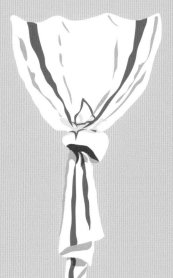

WINDSOCK

An open-sleeve, truncated flag, attached at one end to a ring and pole.

British Library Cataloguing-in-Publication Data.
A CIP record for this book is available from the British Library.

ISBN   978 1 907317 30 9

© 2011 Black Dog Publishing Limited.
All rights reserved.

Black Dog Publishing Limited
10A Acton Street
London
WC1X 9NG

t.   +44 (0)207 713 5097
f.   +44 (0)207 713 8682
e.   info@blackdogonline.com

Black Dog Publishing is an environmentally responsible company. *New Wave: Facts About Flags* is printed on FSC accredited paper.

architecture art design
fashion history photography
theory and things

www.blackdogonline.com

black dog publishing

london uk